Gracie's Corner

*I've Got Something to Say
and I'll Say it My Way…*

Gracie's Corner: I've Got Something to Say and I'll Say it My Way…
Copyright © 2018 by Gracie Lester
Cover by: MRK Publishing
Editor – Michael Ray King
126p. ill. cm.
ISBN 978-1-935795-53-7
LCCN 2018946489

Michael Ray King Publishing
PO Box 353431
Palm Coast, FL 32135-3431

Printed in the United States of America

Acknowledgements

I wish to acknowledge God as the foremost power of my life and His guidance and leadership through my life from birth to now

I would like to acknowledge all the wonderful people I have known who really made my life worthwhile. My mother and father, my grandparents, the Lester and Morgan sides of the family.

Also, my five brothers and five sisters as well as both family sides of uncles, aunts, cousins, nieces and nephews.

I would really feel badly if I left my friends out at West Virginia State University where I am a student. There are so many of you I would spend far too much time and paper space to list you all. You know who you are.

I wish to acknowledge my friends at the Episcopal Church of which I'm a member, as well as the Dunbar Methodist and Presbyterian churches.

I thank each of you for your kindness, support and understanding guidance.

I dedicate this book to the honor of my Mother and Father as well as all my brothers and sisters.

Table of Contents

Domestic Home Engineers or

The Weekly Trash Man

It is Tuesday Morning about 8:00 AM where I live. Promptly at this time I hear the big truck rumbling down the back alley. They're here to pick up yesterday's needs and joys which now have become the junk and trash of each family they visit. The trash men seem unusually happy as they come today, singing, talking and laughing.

I was at the hallway back door peeking out the window to see how much snow had fallen during the night. It appeared to be over the shoes and boots about halfway. The slushy white stuff clung to their boots as more fluttered from the heavens.

The precipitation and cold did not appear to bother these men who knew they had a job that must be done for the people in this area. As they came around the side of the building across from where I live, I could see the long, heavy looking gloves, the big, wide black hat, the dark jacket and the boots that came up to the man's knees. He was riding on the side step of the truck.

He jumped from the truck and sang as he came around the corner of the house. I wasn't sure what he was singing at first, so I opened the door slightly so he could not see me but I could hear.

Joe Moe Doe was singing, "I traced her little foot prints in the snow, the snow. I traced her little foot prints in the snow. God bless that happy day when Nellie lost her way, I found her when the snow was on the ground."

Just about that time the men were at the building where I live. A man jumps out of the right side of the truck and yells to Joe Moe Doe. He asks Joe, "Do you think we can finish gathering up all the trash and get to the dinner at the City Hall in time?"

Joe answers, "Oh sure Charlie! We will have plenty of time to finish our runs in the east end and get back to the garage and freshen up a bit.

A Valentine's Day Dinner prepared by the women of the city is about all I can think of right now!"

Charlie finishes picking up the loose trash on the ground, then he picks up the bags and tosses them into the back of the truck. He places the cans back in the trash bin area upside down. As he is doing this, he says, "I wonder if these people appreciate what we are doing out here in the cold for them. We pick up the garbage and trash on the ground and sometimes the cans are so heavy they feel like their weight is a ton. Sometimes they don't have lids on them so they get full of rain water and snow."

After Charlie finishes placing the cans back where they belong, he yells to Joe who is picking up cans from the house next to this one, "Are you ready to roll Joe?"

"Yeah! Hit the road and get the rest of these places done."

Joe then hollered to the driver, "Gear it up there Billy Bob and let's make a little better time to the other places we must visit!"

"You think it's so much fun being the driver for you two on these weather beaten roads with holes a foot deep in some places. Besides, I could have gotten all that loading done two hours ago!" Billy interjected.

Charlie chimed in, "Ok Billy Bob, you get out here and help us load up a few then you can see what a messy job we work in almost everywhere we stop."

Billy Bob fires up the ignition and he waits for Joe to call Nellie to go with them. Joe whistles and yells, "Here Nellie! Here Nellie! Come on girl, we are ready to move on!"

The cutest little white fluffy dog with small reddish brown spots on its body and on the left ear had a long red area similar to a lopsided "x" or if turned to the right is was more like a cross. Yapping and running, the dog came with a large reddish brown looking dog with an apparent injury to its left eye. The dog had a limp when walking on the right front leg. I could not determine from where I was standing what might have caused the injury, but an educated guess was possible it had been shot with a BB gun causing both injuries and maybe both sides.

Charlie got out of the truck and looked at the larger dog examining the eye then the right side of the body. He realized right away these were injuries done some time ago to the animal, probably causing a lot of arthritic pains when walking. It was obvious the animal had a serious visual disability of the left eye.

He turned to Nellie and said, "He is a very nice play mate for you, but he belongs to someone else so we can't take him with us. See he has a collar on and there is a telephone number for us to call to get his master."

Just then a lady walked around the corner and said, "Thank God you found him. I thought he had wandered off and couldn't find his way back since he is visually impaired. The snow is causing his vision to be worse. Thank you so much, all of you, for being so kind to him. I am Hazel Adams and I live over on the sixth street. He is usually a good dog, but will wander away at times and gets lost."

Charlie then introduces himself, and Joe does the same. Bill gets out of the truck and introduces himself. They learn from talking to Mrs. Adams that her husband works for the state in the tax department. Mrs. Adams had a small purse with her and had some scrap paper in it.

She gave each of them her telephone number saying, "Please call after 5:00 in the evening. My husband Roy would love to thank you also. Homer is his whole life. You see, my husband has a disability also and is wheel chair bound most of the time from Multiple Sclerosis."

Mrs. Adams helped Homer get into the Jeep Cherokee and they drove away. Charlie, Joe, and Bill got into the city sanitation truck and drove on to the remainder of the houses they needed to visit. Charlie had Nellie sitting next to him.

He tugged at her left ear and said, "Nellie, he was very nice but a little too big for you. It's all right for you to hunt for a boyfriend, but be careful and selective."

They completed the homes they ordinarily visited once a week and performed Domestic Home Engineers duties. Charlie. Joe, Bill and Nellie were getting very hungry, thirsty and needed a pit stop. They were on their way back down the road down a back alley close to the upper end of Dunbar at an old house which had been abandoned for several years.

The older couple who owned the property had been placed in a nursing home. The three children of the couple had left this area after finishing college to other states to get better employment to take care of their families and did not wish to return. As they were driving along down the back alley, Charlie yelled for Bill to stop. He could see something over on the right that looked strange.

It was up over a little knoll where there were no immediate houses. They all three got out of the truck and went toward the object. As they got closer Charlie said. "It looks like a mannequin that women use when they sew to keep the garment straight while they work on it."

Then as they got closer they could see it was a human body lying on a mattress of some type with a blanket and quilt over it. Before they got close enough to recognize she was probably dead, they could hear a baby crying faintly. As they proceeded nearer, Bill got on the truck cell phone and notified Emergency Medical Services and the police.

Charlie and Joe checked and realized the woman was apparently dead as they could get no pulse. Charlie picked the baby up. He opened his jacket to put it inside to receive the warmth from his body. He then closed his jacket to keep the wind and cold out.

 Joe and Bill checked the woman to see if she might still be breathing. They found what appeared to be a large amount of fresh blood from her vaginal area to her breast. That's where Charlie had found the baby laying and picked it up to protect it until the paramedics arrived.

The paramedics were on the scene almost immediately. So was the local police department of Dunbar. The Drug Team was notified and they moved on the scene very quickly.

On investigation by the police of the area, there was evidence the lady was from Kentucky, but once had some family who lived in this area. Charlie graciously handed the tiny baby girl over to the paramedics and said. "Take care of her. She is very special to me."

The baby was taken to a local hospital. After examination by the paramedics, the body of the lady was taken to the State Medical Coroner's office. The police chief looked at Joe, Charlie and Billy Bob and said, "That was a very good job by all three of you men. We need more just like you. Hurry along now and you can still get some of that Valentine's Day food the women made. They are serving right now at the city building for the city employees. I telephoned them and they are warming it up. They also have some special goodies for you.

Written Monday 4/29/2010

The Rock of Life

Sometimes in my mind, I wander back because of something else I've read or heard someone say which reminds me of a faint memory of my past, This is one of those days when 1 find myself thinking a lot about my oldest brother, Stacy.

I think I was either three or four years old. I am just not really clear on that, but other happenings in my life around that time seems to persuade me to go in that direction of time. I recall my family lived in a large house probably about one half mile away from the main highway. The property sported a small stream of water which the local people called a creek.

There also was a road which led to a bridge that crossed a river to the main highway. This led to the Red Jacket Coat Company on the right. On the left stood a small town called Baileysville. The small stream of water which passed the house led into the main river.

Our viewing area is where we often sat watching people walking up and down the road on horseback or with their dog. This area was a long porch, which extended from one end of the house to the other. On the left as we faced the road, the porch curled around the house to a door which led into the main living room.

We could also see the embankment with many rocky cliff areas from the stream of water leading straight up to the road. In my mind's eye now, it seems I can see the cliffs as being up much higher than us from our view point. In the back of the house was an area with thick bushes on one side and high rocks on the other but not so high the skilled person could not jump across them without problems.

One day my sister Eileen, brother Stacey, and I were up among the rocks playing. Eileen and Stacey started the game of jumping across the rocks to the other side.

Stacey said "let's see who can jump from side to side and make it ok."

The game started and Stacey jumped first, full of graceful movement and balance and ample space to spare. Eileen then took her turn and went across with space to spare on the other side.

When it was my turn I started to cry and backed away from the jump area. I was frightened. That area below me, when peeking down, was very deep. They both reached out their hands and urged me to get closer to the edge and don't look down. Instead, they pleaded, I was to look straight ahead and grab their hands as I got closer to the edge.

I tried. I was so small. My arms and hands could not meet theirs and I fell. The area was really not a deep space at all but to my mind's eye at that time it was a terrible fall.

My brother jumped into the rocky area with me. He picked me up and checked to see if I was all right. He then told Eileen he would get me started by pushing me up the rock. She needed to brace her feet on the rock with the split edge and part of it higher than the other.

He told her, "When I push Gracie up, you reach out your hands and pull her up while I push her for the top. It was a tug of war, so to speak, for Eileen and Stacey to help me up the rocks. I was resisting them so much, still frightened and crying with a few bruises from the fall, but nothing serious,

My brother finally yelled out at me, "Gracie! Stop fighting us! We are trying to help you get that tub of lard on up there when I push you or I'll let you hit rock bottom again!"

Needless to say, but I will, that's all it took to get me to move on up to where Eileen could reach my hands and help to pull me up.

Written Monday 9/l4/2009

Gracie, Why are you Growing Old?

Recently, I was visiting in the home of friends where a small child, a boy four-years-old was visiting with his mother and other family members. It was a good visit for me in many ways as I got to see some people I had not seen a lot of since they moved from this area.

Several family members were there and a few friends besides me. We talked about many things and then when I got ready to leave. I went around to all the small children to give them a hug. The best comment I could think of was to make them realize I still remembered them.

One of the small boys sitting on the couch stood up and offered me his right hand to shake instead of a hug. Then he looked up at me and said, "Gracie? Why are you growing old?"

I was startled to say the least to get a comment like that from a child who just turned four years of age two weeks ago. I was muttering and trying hard to find the right words to say to a child that age to answer his question.

Several persons in the room, mainly his teenage cousins and aunts said, "Dennis, you are growing, old too."

I could see the child wanted an answer from me to be satisfied. His mother was sitting in the computer chair at the computer across the room. I muttered and looked at his mother with a sigh of desperation. I turned my back slightly and asked his mother what she would approve of me telling him?

She softly said, "He asked you the question so you should answer the question."

I then turned back to the child and said, "Dennis, when your mother and father decided they wanted you and asked God to help them, the moment you were created you started to get old. And the moment you were born on this earth, you started to get old faster than when your parents was making you. Therefore live your life to the fullest, Dennis. Use what you learn with whatever your parents, grandparents, other family members, friends, your church family, the schools you will be attending, and any other activities you will be in with your friends teaches you throughout your life. Remember, Dennis, you are only four-years-old and I am seventy-seven. You have a long way to go before you will get old and have snow white hair, wrinkles on your face, brown spots on your hands and legs, and get Arthritis pains when you sit in one position too long. Have fun and enjoy your life through every phase and change as you live it. Remember life is a gift from God, your mother and father. Try to create your own faith, hope, and love as you live your life. Reach back from time to time with your faith, hope, and love and help those who are less fortunate than you. For in doing this you will become a much wiser person who has made peace with yourself, God, and the universe. Did I answer your question Dennis? Do you now understand why I am growing old?"

It is the natural process of life from when our parents first made us, to our birth, through our life to our death or when we go back to God.

Yes, Dennis told me he understood. He gave me a big hug when I got down to his level. To tell you the truth he got a couple of good strong hugs as well.

Written Thursday 2/4/2010

Dear Father

Today, I am in my senior citizen years looking back on some of the very good memories I have of my childhood and my father. I thought and reflected many times on the decision of how I would write this memoir of my dad.

At long last I decided l would write you a work of art somewhat like a letter. In memories that I have of you, I have chosen one which is profound in my mind.

When I was a child about eight-years-old I can remember early one morning on a Saturday when dad was coming home from work. My dad was a coal miner and he worked the night shift, therefore at about nine-ten that morning he got home.

On this particular day it was summertime and the month I do not re-call. My older sister, brother, myself, and Helen, my younger sister at that time, heard him singing and whistling as he came down the mountain near the little knoll where we lived.

Suddenly there was a mad scramble of feet, laughter, and loud talking as the four of us ran toward the singing and whistling. My brother and older sister got there first, greeting my dad who was standing in the middle of the road. Rhododendron bushes grew along both sides of where he stood. He happily and joyously grabbed Eileen and Stacey giving them a big hug. Then I came puttering along to get my moment of gladness and a hug from him.

Back down the hill, Helen came with tears in her eyes and crying because she couldn't go any faster. My dad saw her tears and he walked slowly to her. He picked her up consoled her by talking to her, then handed her a little brown bag with several different kinds of candy. He then gave the three of us standing nearby the same.

My dad had the habit of stopping once or twice a week at the Red Jacket Coal Company grocery store in Wyoming County on the way home from work to buy several kinds of candy.

He would then divide the sweets into the four bags for us. This was a practice my father had which still remains in my memories of him.

His singing and whistling of "She'll be Coming Round the Mountain When She Comes" makes me very sentimental when I remember my dad. Seeing him standing there among those beautiful blooming white, pink, purple, and even colors I cannot remember of Rhododendron bushes leave s a breath-taking magical moment for me.

Written Friday 9/11 /2009

Daddy's Cap

I do not recall the exact time for the remembrance of this story in my life. I think it was possibly when I was four or five years of age. I just re-call I must have been very difficult with a lot of whining and my mother couldn't seem to get me satisfied.

I was indeed, during this time of my life, a very active child, never staying still in one place of the house for a very long period of time. When doing my house explorations on this particular day I found my dad's coal miner cap he wore when he went into the mines to work to protect his head from loose coal that might be falling.

Coal miners lowered their heads when on the small vehicle used to get them down into the working area of the ground. From there they dig the coal and send it back to the surface to be processed and sent to proper places for inspection before going to market. I put the cap on my head and my mother showed me the switch in the front and how to turn it on and off to get the light. I remember I found some letters on the side of the cap and I asked my mother what they were.

She told me that it spelled CARBIDE. I wanted her to explain to me what that meant. She told me that's the company that makes the caps to protect your daddy's head when he goes into the mines to work.

I looked again with a sense of question at the black cap with a strap to fasten it around the neck and the word written in white CARBIDE. Then, I put the cap on my head and asked my mother to fasten the strap and I took off running through the house flipping the light on and off. My mother called out as I ran past her with one of her favorite sayings to me, "Don't get hurt my Little Angel, while down in the mines. I'll see you when you get home!"

Written Friday 9/11/2009

It's Not So Bad Growing Old

When I decided on this title on which to write a memoir, it took some time for me to get the stream of thoughts flowing so I could write it in some sensible manner. I realized after much thinking just to relax as I write. Everything is a part of life whether good or bad, happy or sad, jubilant or depressing. We all have our own measure of each of these to face and get through.

I often have heard from the old folks it's God's way of testing your strength for the next assignment he has for you to do. He just gives you a little time along the way to rest, re-invigorate your strength, cleanse your spiritual house then start on a clean slate. This way, you get to build your goals quite often in a different direction. The new one will possibly be better for you.

Many times I have remembered an old saying my Grandmother Morgan would repeat to my brothers, sisters and I – "Change was good for the spirit and soul." It helps to make you a better person with a keen sharp mind from past experiences good and bad to be a better you. Often the old mountain sayings of people I've known and respected have guided me through tremulous times of worry, anxiety, fear, danger, frustrations, disappointment and much more.

But memories of my family, Lester, Morgan, and many very good friends in the past enhanced the teachings of those persons to give me a much better sense of what survival should mean to all of us. I learned how we reach the height of survival in a very chaotic world with very bad economic times for many persons.

Yes indeed, to all who read this. I wish to say now, "IT'S NOT SO BAD GROWING OLD!" For in the growing old you can look back and reflect on the broader picture to see the errors more clearly and think about the ways you managed them.

You may think more clearly on the causative factors of those problems, some of which you might have been responsible for happening. Even those you've had a more controlled and regulated process of growing, as in medical help, or psychological or psychiatric therapy.

I have had several of these controlled and regulated processes and I feel they have helped me a lot to be what I am today. So you see my friends. "IT'S NOT SO BAD GROWING OLD!" You still make memories as you go. Many that help you in your ongoing growth and development of life.

Written Tuesday 9/15/2009

Mystery of the Library Pin

Recently on a Sunday after church services, I was shopping at Kroger's in Dunbar, WV. I was moving around slowly from place to place looking for the items I had on my List. As what is normal for me, I get involved in looking at a lot of food items, mainly reading the labels.

I am checking for their price, the size of the item such as a can of food the size in ounces or whatever. I also check for the date of best buy and expiration date for buying. Another big item for me is the nutritional value of what I am checking. I want to know the calorie count, fat, salt, carbohydrates, sugar, proteins, vitamins, and minerals, plus many other food contents that might affect my health in some way if they are high.

For example, if I have a blood pressure problem, I have been taught to keep the salt level of foods canned, or otherwise, to below 600mgm for each meal. If I have snacks I know I must count the salt level on those also and keep a written level in order to maintain good health habits with the use of foods.

I do this with all of the major food level problem makers such as fats, sugar, carbohydrates, proteins and others when I am shopping to get the best nutritional foods for my health issues to use in cooking. On the Sunday that I was shopping and doing so using the previously listed process, I was deep in concentration on my shopping duties.

I remember I perceived there was a presence of another person near me and out of the corner of my eye I could see it was a lady. I didn't think very much about it and went right on checking the foods I was selecting and placing in the grocery cart.

Suddenly there was a position change of the lady and myself, which brought us face to face. I remember she was slightly taller than me and I am 5 feet and 4 inches tall. She had a big smile on her face and was looking at what I thought was the necklace I was wearing.

Her eyes had a warm friendly expression and really, I thought she looked like someone I had known in the past but could not get her name to come to me.

She looked directly into my eyes again with those eyes of hazel blue, smiled and even her face was creating an image I thought I should know. She then said, "I have noticed many times you wear that pin which says, 'I Support Libraries.'"

I was indeed startled to hear her make a comment like that. I had carefully been looking at her trying to determine in my mind who she could be. I was fascinated with the clothes she was wearing. In my mind I was thinking, WOW! Who is she married to or who is her male friend that can afford to buy clothes like that for her? They looked like none other than Macy's or from some place in New York, Chicago or some other large shopping area for clothes.

I then became a little more aware of what she had said to me and I thought, "Oh No! She is going to tell me I can't wear the pin unless I am officially and legally the spokesperson for libraries.

I then looked her straight in those hazel blue eyes with the intent of telling her I have been an ardent fan of libraries since I was at Pineville High School. The principle at the school arranged for one of my classmates, Emily, and I, to work as student assistants to help the school librarians gather up the books left on the tables and to clean the tables that often were left a little in need.

We were allowed to help the librarians to put the books in their proper places in the library. The principal of the school at the time was Mr. Jess Houck, who arranged for Emily and I to receive minimal wages for the work we did to help the school librarians for three days a week.

This was the greatest class in Library Science I have ever had. It was so much fun working with Emily and the library staff and this was my first official job earning money. The lady did not say anything to me about the library pin as I thought she would. Instead, before she left where we were standing, she asked me why I wore the pin?

I explained to her a friend at the church I attend gave it to me when the Kanawha Valley area had the levy a few years ago to get money to be able to keep the libraries functioning. This way they could do the things they always had done in the past for the babies, children, teenagers, adults, those with disabilities, and seniors and much more for the people of the Kanawha Valley area.

The friend also gave me a large number of leaflets explaining all about the levy and why it was necessary now as they were no longer covered by the professional group that had helped them. She explained I could wear the pin if I chose to go around to neighbors, friends, and others and ask them to help the libraries by voting for the levy on a specific date. I did as the friend requested and passed all the leaflets out to very kind and helpful persons who made very special and kind remarks about the pin I wore.

After this discussion with the lady she looked at me again with those hazel blue eyes and said, "Do you like reading and how does reading relate to the language of the words in the books?"

I didn't know how to answer at first and was somewhat perplexed of where to start. I slowly looked at her and in a stumbling voice I said, "My concept of language is anything we hear, see, perceive, touch, feel, and understand as it is processed in our brain is the use of language and or words. The power of this language is the ability of animals, people, and any type of life that can use it to help them in their survival techniques all over the universe. I believe no one sector of persons, animals, nor does any form of life own this power. It is a gift from God."

She smiled and I could feel the understanding and warmth in her eyes as she said, "PERFECT." then turned and walked away. I stood watching as she strolled away and it took several minutes for me to collect my senses of what she meant.

Written Tuesday 9/1/2011

Tomorrow Is Just Today a Little Further Away (two poems)

The Dream

Tomorrow is just today a little further away

How can we see or understand?

What that will bring for the dreams we had

Yet it's so true we still visualize

Our hearts sing out a song of goodwill

Only trust me and this I will bring

Then you will see the truth to behold

Life's happy journey together grow old

For as long as you live when the truth you see

Will continue on into eternity

Happiness

Today, tomorrow, forever

I will sing a love song to you.

Then you will know and understand

Dreams that we wove you will see

The answer tomorrow today I give

Heart songs we sing of joy and goodwill.

My faith and trust I leave unto you

Behold the truth I bring unto you

Life's journey together in life will be

As long as we wish to eternity.

Written Thursday 3/11/2010

Were Those Tears?

Were those tears I saw in your eyes or just the reflection of mine own heart?

Whatever starts it I don't know the river of tears I have sometimes

From my eyes to the nose and chin and then dropping down on my clothes

Somehow there is a spark of the past filling the air with its perfume

A brief memory of dreams lost in the passing of its living

Only time can help me see the truth of all the dreams.

It is better I say to myself to learn to let it go

To plan and build a better rhythm of life for myself

For others who were involved its best I do it this way

For yesterday's dreams were just a mist of happy things to be

But never made the passing score of truly good folklore

They were lived and now passed away into eternity,

Therefore my friends as we speak today on the road of life

What are those tears I see in your eyes or is it just a reflection

Of the mist of the life I lived long ago and it still visits me at times

To remind me once it was real, but couldn't be anymore

The circumstances of that time forced us apart

To nevermore be as it was then to live into eternity.

To you my friends and foes alike I say let's both become wiser

For the living of life with more caution and placing the guard for oneself

Experience I have heard is always the best teacher

I hope it helps us all in the moments when we are weaker

I bid farewell to you all in this writing of my living

Live your life to the best of your ability and time will give you your answer.

I see your tears from time to time but only in a mist

I know you suffer much like I in those days long ago

But time has helped the passing of the sharpness and the pain

Now I see the picture and the story much more clearly

Giving understanding and joy to see the picture

Time has given to all involved happiness, peace and joy.

I've learned its best to live in peace, love and
harmony

Life is too short for all of us to always place
the blame

It's better to gather the sheaves of life move on
and try again

In time the maze of everything lost will fade
and pass away

You will realize it's gone and now you're free
to live once more

At times with mists of these words you are
forgiven and I am forgiven,

Written Monday 5/10/2010

I Found It

I have many things to say to you but for now
you would not understand

For a little while you will not see me nor
understand, but only trust

For a little while and you will see me and
understand

The truth will come and will guide you into all
that is real

When I return your sorrow and pain shall turn
to joy

Much as a woman who is in her hour of travail
will have great sorrow

Because her hour has come for the birth of the
child

After the child has been delivered she forgets
the pain and anguish

And rejoices with great happiness of the birth
of the child

In this life it is so often a reality for man to just
live the best he can

Caring for his own providing their needs

Sharing if he can for those not as fortunate

The peace of life will he with all who learn to
trust

And live the golden rule of life, love thy
neighbor as thyself

I have found it, the spirit of caring, forgiving
and living life to its fullest

The best that I can do in every way

When night time comes remember those most
in need to the spirit

And ask the Spirit and the Son to intercede to
the Father for their needs

When morning comes and I awaken, it seems
there is an atmosphere of peace and
contentment.

A kind of peace that makes me realize God heard my prayers and he is working on them.

I have found it as life goes on, the peace, understanding and contentment I need.

Written Tuesday 4/13/2010

The Skate Board Man

Down he goes to the street below long hair
flowing in the wind as he goes

He gazes about from side to side looking at the
houses with great pride.

Arms reaching out hands straight as he moves
sounds from his mouth of words said

Oh, how I wish that his words I could hear
when his look at the houses seem so real.

The voices I hear as I walk so near he never
turns not even a stare

It seems he has his focus fixed on something
that is dear to him.

It seems in his stance as he looks straight ahead
he has found peace with the wind

Hoping the story the wind tells him will
someday become real.

And understands in time he will know the truth and peace of it all

That his hopes, dreams, happiness and joy will all become a part of him,

He likes the feel of the wind in his hair he understands each change and he cares

The wind is the master leading him to the possibility that it will all be true.

Finding at the end of his riveting ride a moment of justice and joy at his side

Somehow he knew deep in his heart time would give him a chance to be.

Looking around to see how his friends came through the process of mercy to fend

His friends he knows will all do well trusting like he of the given promise.

Laughter, joking and happy delay, they wait for their friends and report a good day

Friends of his seem to be happy laughing and talking about this day,

Each one giving his version of the excitement and exhilaration of their latest ride

This I hear as I am walking near feeling great
pride for the young men's day.

Riding standing and sometimes sitting either
way they fly through the air

Young men willing to learn balance knowing
they will earn the happiness they seek.

Right on into late evening they ride often alone
and sometimes beside

It gives me pleasure to recognize young men
like these often become great men.

Other friends that join their parade they glide
together in precision unafraid

Each one knowing that tomorrow will bring
another day to practice and gain,

More courage, strength and preciseness each
day they know that life will give

The best to each man as life goes on who
practice and follow the rules.

Each time I see them I know that will be a fact
of reality for them

Perfection and honor becomes with practice in
time to the weakest of men.

A proper balance of peace and happiness will come slowly to you

But you will recognize it was because you practiced and followed the rules.

Written Thursday 5/6/2010

Promises Broken

You promised me the moon in all its glorious
seasons

I got a garden of vegetables to tend

Now you are gone the wind whispers to me

You left for another farther away.

I have a deep sadness slowly at times

Wondering if it was planned all the time

But just as quickly as it comes

It passes and is gone, but never to stay.

You promised me the sun to brighten my day

I got buckets of tears for my vegetable garden

Dark clouds gather the rains come down

Rivers over flow and moisture abounds.

You promised me love in the sweet by and by

But now I realize it was all just a lie

Maybe you meant it to be true at first

But then after knowing me you just took foot and left.

The sounds I hear in the wind by day

Tell me you ponder the treasures of life today

Perhaps if we could as humans just see and know

How to better the life of the other they would find a way.

Written Thursday 2/18/2010

Looking to the Future

In this section or my memoir, I find myself questioning why in some sense I returned to college. Thirty-eight years have passed since I've been in this type setting. I clearly tell myself this is a dream I've had for all those years. I had to just suppress it and handle life as it was at the moment for survival reasons.

At that time, I was dealing with many very personal health issues some of which were serious and others of not a serious nature. I had used all the money I had saved for the project and was not eligible for any of the funds available in those days.

Therefore, again it became necessary for me to return to work as a Registered Nurse for survival reasons. When once it was supposed to be a degree in education and eventually to teach children in the first, second, or third grades, I have now decided at 76 years of age it might be more profitable for me to choose Language Arts and Creative Writing.

The first master piece of writing was penned by me when I was eight years old. As the years went on I did other writings which seemed to satisfy my need to express in the written word what I could not relate or say in reality.

Now one of my purposes of what I am doing is for it to become profitable for me in years to come. I decided if I am going to spend a lot of time and effort in doing something like this, I want to learn how to do it the professional way. Thus began the process of working through the different requirements of WV State University to get readmitted as a student. This is a positive step for me.

So far all has gone well for me with the assistance of a lot of great people all over the university campus. I have been greatly assisted in my quest for the required re-admission activities.

The initial reality of studies, papers due, reading assignments, and parking problems haven't bothered me very much. So far I've only been late for class one time for fifteen minutes and part of it was my fault for having that extra cup of coffee. I sheepishly left my home in Dunbar seven minutes later than usual. The traffic flow down the road from where I live was moving a little slower than usual for needed reasons. Right now, except for the initial shocks, I seem to be adjusting very well. I am enjoying taking classes with the young people as well as the older students like me.

I am beginning to realize this is just all a part of life. In anything new or different in life we do adjustments are required. The sad part of a lot of this to me is I lost a lot of work I had written and saved through the years in a house fire in 1981. I think I can still remember most of it.

In time, with the help of the very good professors presently working with me and those yet to come in classes I will be taking, the words will come back to my memory.

My goal is to remember as much as possible - the times, ages, subject material - and get it into writing again in a positive, professional manner for my future wherever I am and whatever I'm doing. Only God and time knows the answer to that. All good things for me will be in God's Time.

Written Wednesday, 9/16/2009

A Special Conference with Pearl Buck

Recently, I attended a conference at West Virginia State University celebrating the Humanitarian Legacy of Pearl S. Buck. It was presented by The College of Business and Social Sciences by three instructors of West Virginia State University. Dr. Michael E. Workman opened the discussion and introduced the other two speakers from the university. He also welcomed everyone to the conference including the keynote speaker, Mr. Kirk Judd.

Dr. Billy Joe Peyton, Professor of History of West Virginia State University gave "A Glimpse of Pearl Bucks Life." As the daughter of a missionary family who lived in China most of their life, her parents took her and two brothers there when she was just a small child.

Dr. T.J. Park, instructor of the History Department, discussed some of the many activities Pearl Buck did after she moved back to America. Buck returned to the United States to be near her small daughter who had a disability. The young child had been placed in a special facility where she would be protected and taken care of for the rest of her life.

Pearl Buck divorced her husband in China and married her Editor, John Walsh. Walsh managed the writing and editing of her work and other business details.

Pearl Buck became very famous as a world renowned person. She worked and assisted with the principles of helping persons with disabilities such as seniors, babies, and children. She focused on better health, education, living conditions and any other assets of improved life for them and their families. One of her books titled, "My Several Worlds" relates to the activities she worked so hard to get for people she came in contact with and their needs.

Dr. Park also discussed many other activities Ms. Buck was involved with trying to make conditions better for the people. Another of these activities was with the many Asian children fathered by the soldiers in the war times of Korea, Vietnam, and other places in Asia such as Japan. When the men left the areas after the war was over, the children and their mothers were left with no father for the child. The mother was left to raise the children alone.

A lot was done for these individuals but because of the difficulty of getting green cards for the mothers to get to America with the child, many cases became a big frustration for Pearl Buck and those who worked with her. She never stopped working until her dying day of 80 years of age. She continued diligently trying to do more for these abandoned families. The situation remains a problem even today.

Many places such as libraries and parks were named to honor Pearl Buck. She left her own personal legacy to many people in her writing of books, essays, articles and other work about them.

Ms. Buck suffered many disappointments of not being able to do as she wanted to do for the distressed people. She was often blocked by politics and legislation by congress in America. When she died, Ms. Buck had much to be proud of in her work both in America and in the many countries where she traveled. She helped people wherever she went and made life better for them.

The final speaker was Kirk Judd who is the appointed person in charge of "Pearl Buck's Commitment to West Virginia and Her Birth Place." He told us this has been an ongoing activity since her death in 1973. The group who work with Mr. Judd have bought the land and the home of her birth place and much of the items from family and friends which was in the home at the time the family left as missionary's to China. They are refurbishing the inside and outside of the home to be the way it was then. The house is now on the National Register of Historic Places. We may visit, view, and take pictures, much as they would any other such property of special memories to honor Pearl Buck and all she meant to the United States and the world. Pearl Bucks birth place is located in Hillsboro, Pocahontas County, West Virginia.

Pearl Buck began her writing career with the writing and publication of "East Wind: West Wind" in 1930. The book was made into a movie but I do not remember exactly when this happened. I can't remember what Mr. Judd said. Her next book, "The Good Earth," won the 1932 Pulitzer Prize. She won The Nobel Peace Prize for Literature of 1938. She went on to win many prizes over the years for her written books, articles, essays, and many other different types of writing. She wrote 85 books altogether and 100 works of fiction and non-fiction in her life time.

I personally had the privilege of meeting Pearl Buck not very long before she died. She visited the former Diamond Department Store in Charleston, West Virginia. I cannot remember exactly the date. I know it was in the spring time and about the middle of April. I think it was about 1968 or 1969. 1 read about her plans for coming to Charleston and saw it on the evening news.

She was on the top floor autographing her books and meeting the people of the multi-purpose area which was usually the dining area of the Diamond Department Store. I remember I was a wee bit late getting there but it didn't matter as there was a long line of people ahead of me waiting to meet her and get their books signed.

Suddenly, I was getting too warm as I had worn a heavy dress since it was still quite cool outside. I also was wearing a long coat down below my knees. I started to remove the coat and I could see her even from the distance looking at me and she said, "don't take the coat off, it is very becoming to you and I like it."

The coat was black with several sections of white around the collar, the front down form the arm pits to the hem line. I don't remember where I got it but I think it was either Good Will in Charleston, W.V. or Indianapolis or possibly Lane Bryant's in Indianapolis as I shopped a lot with them. I left the coat on and eventually I worked myself up to where she autographed my "Good Earth" and "My Several World" books. I noticed she did not rush anyone and spoke very softly and kind. She had something special to say to all of us. She looked up from where she was seated with those big blue eyes and made very special comments to all of us as we worked our way through.

Written Tuesday 10/25/2016

The Dog Wood Tree Journey

I begin this article by saying I love to watch babies at play and when they mingle with other children. It seems to be their way of communicating when I see them reaching for a favorite toy, an animal, or for a person they recognize, respect, and want to make their means of communication. Especially, if the baby is about eight months to one year and sometimes even earlier they can amaze me with their attempts of their first words, touch to get your attention, and of course other ways they have been taught by family members or learned by watching and listening to family members.

I remember in my family many times when an older sister or brother would say words within hearing distance of a younger child my mother did not like the sound of and she would first give us that mother look which we all learned as we grew older meant, "don't speak those words in front of the baby." And, if that didn't get our attention to her satisfaction then we could expect her to come with the switch or ground us to a room with the door closed for the length of time she thought was adequate for the punishment.

Once my older brother looked at a baby sister when our mother was changing her diaper and she was about seven months old. My brother grabbed his nose and covered it, "saying my goodness Dew Drop, (Fake Name) can't you do better than that? You are going to stink us all out of here with all that mess (fake word) used out of respect of those who prefer the use of more professional words.

I can remember in my own growth and development that there were some problems at times that I would hear my mother telling an older sibling to stop talking to me in whatever the situation was in regards to our socializing in jump rope, playing tag you are it or testing who could run the fastest and the amount of distance.

But there were also the times that we played games together and learned very good lessons from our older brother and sister of having a very good learning experience together of safety and security.

I remember once when I was about eight years old my oldest brother challenged me to climb a Dog Wood tree after he had done so. Fortunately for me the tree was not very tall and there was a pile of sand and a few gravels of broken rock near the sand pile. After, he came down I started trying to climb the tree by placing my feet bare footed as he told me to do. It was rough climbing, but I couldn't let my bother think he was the only one that could climb a Dog Wood tree. I kept placing my feet a little higher as I went, but I could feel them getting painful like the skin was broken. Once I looked down and I could see why.

One foot looked like it was bleeding. I could see the blood and I began to freak out screaming at my brother. I was so mad at him I stopped concentrating on how he had taught me the safe way to climb the tree, and keep the proper balance as I went. I let go of one limb and the other one was not strong enough to hold me alone. The next thing I knew, I was falling and my body hit the sand pile. Then, I felt some blood oozing from right side of my head and then I passed out completely.

My brother screamed for my mother and dad to come and help him get me on my feet. Instead, after they saw me, my dad got a blanket from the house and one for under my head. They cleaned me as necessary and finally got me to respond enough to be able to walk to get to the house with them holding me up as necessary. Then my dad went to my uncle's house who lived the closest and had a car.

They took me to the only doctor in the area near and he treated me as he could, then by ambulance I was taken to Stevens Clinic Hospital in Welch, West Virginia where I stayed for two weeks for observation and care for possible brain injury.

I learned a good lesson from all of that. I never took any more dares from my brother again to do the same things he could do so easily and not get hurt. Neither did I ever try to climb Dog Wood tree again. Instead in the spring time when they are in full bloom, I just look at them and admire their beauty and what they represent in life.

Written Monday 9/12/2016

The Strength of Motivation

The strength of motivation is very important in the planning and structure of almost anything we do in life. It may take time to realize this as we decide what we want to do and plan the details of it. As we progress in the planning and doing this will all be more clearly seen and understood.

Several years ago this became a reality to me more when I decided I wanted to learn to drive and get my first car. I was already 66 years old when I retired as a practicing Professional Registered Nurse and had never driven on the main roads.

The only experience I had in driving was my oldest brother taught me how to drive on country roads where one hardly ever met another vehicle except about every five miles or more. He started by having me to look down at the brakes and driving pedals and made me repeat to him what each of these were. It was a little hard for me to see and understand what he was saying at first, therefore he urged me to get on my knees to see inside the car.

When I protested this was hurting my knees he urged me to squat down and look inside the car where the feet would be then he began his discussion. Then he continued by showing me the steering wheel and explained its purpose. He showed me the area where I would see how many miles I was going and how much gas I had in the vehicle.

He then said, "that's all you really need to know except just put your right foot on the brake, the key in the ignition and turn the car on. After doing that slowly take your foot off the brake and very lightly place it on the gas pedal."

I thought I was following his instructions right down to the T. Apparently my understanding of lightly place your foot on the gas was not the same as his meaning and understanding. The car jerked and went forward so fast I almost fainted right there. My brother screamed out and used one of his choice cuss words saying, "Are you trying to get us both killed, Gracie. I told you to very lightly put your foot on the gas pedal and press down very slowly and light giving this car a signal you are going to drive it, but will start slowly."

He then told me to get out of the car and come to the side where he was seated and he would sit at the driver's seat and show me what he was explaining to me. We did the seat exchange and he did as he said he would do then drove the car about a mile or so to allow me to relax. We then did the seat exchange again and the driving went a little more natural for me.

I was not frightened anymore until I saw a vehicle coming in the distance which looked like a big truck loaded with logs. I asked my brother what to do as I was in the center of the road driving right toward that big truck with the logs. He told me to drive over to the right side of the road and stop until the truck passed us then go right back into the center of the road and keep driving.

"You won't meet another car or truck for five miles or so down the road again so there is nothing for you to worry about except look straight ahead and keep your foot on the gas."

It was almost as he had said, but not quite. About ten minutes after the big truck with logs passed us here comes a car driving very fast down the road and I almost freaked out. This time my brother was gentler and calmly said, "don't get scared Gracie. I will help you with the steering wheel and we will bring the car over to the right side of the road together."

We did as he said, and the fast driving car passed us with what appeared to be a man driving and a lady sitting beside him in squalling pain. According to the man as he drove by she was having labor pains and he was trying to get her to the nearest doctor's office for assistance in delivering the baby. My brother yelled out at him, "ok, buddy. Hope you make it in time." My brother could see I was almost as nervous and ready to scream as the woman in the car in labor pains. He told me we should change seats again and he would try it again someday when I felt I was ready to go through all these type of episodes.

The time was never available again as he had been accepted into the Marine Corp. and left about two weeks after my first lesson. I had already graduated from high school and had been accepted into the school of nursing at the Former Charleston General Hospital School of Nursing. He left before I did for the Marine Corp and I left the first week of August 1952 for Charleston, WV.

Three more very busy years passed while I was a student nurse at the Former Charleston General Hospital School of Nursing. After I graduated from there and took the state license Board Examination passing it and officially became a Registered Nurse, I spent one year at Charleston General Hospital working as a Registered Nurse then moved to Man, WV and worked in the newly formed Coal Miners Hospital where I could make more money for college for a year.

I then moved to Indianapolis, Indiana where 1 spent six years at the Indiana University Extension Center, working in a hospital and getting my degree as a Professional Registered Nurse with a BS Degree in General Nursing. I worked there at differential hospitals for another period of time before I moved back to the Kanawha Valley area and worked at several different job places always dreaming of the time when I could save enough money to take driving lessons from an official driving instructor. I was so tired of having to take cabs, bus's, or depend on neighbors or nurse friends to take me to and from work, doctors appointment, and other places. I vowed before I was to old I would learn how to drive and get my first car.

Most job places where I worked, I didn't earn enough money to make any big adventures such as taking official driving lessons nor to buy a car. Finally, after several tries I was accepted for employment at the Former West Virginia Rehabilitation Center. While working there the Director of Nurses when I first started taught me a few very good lessons on how to save money.

I started with her advice to placing $5.00 dollars every two weeks as we received our pay checks in the Credit Union. By the time I was ready to retire I had more than ten thousand dollars saved. The Rehabilitation Center also had a personal account that could be matched by the state, if we did not use all of our vacation and sick leave time. I refrain from saying the exact amount I was given when I first retired and the credit union amount as a total was put into a CD at the bank I do business with.

I was retired by this time and I was still working at the Former West Virginia Rehabilitation Center part time as needed, which worked out well in my favor as many persons did not care for working with those type patients.

I located a professional driving instructor and started my official on the real road with many vehicles instructions. There was a delay after about two months of lessons as my instructor could not legally give me further instructions until I had eye surgery in both eyes due to cataracts. This took about ten months for the two surgery's and the recuperation before he would let me go back on the open road.

Finally, I did get back on the open road and completed my lessons and other requirements, and bought my first car October 11, 2001. I will say there has been some problems with one train, one car incident, and one car hit the driver's car door of my car, but we worked it all out with my insurance company.

Due to my age now I am not as brave as when I first started driving by myself in 2001 and got my first car. But, I am very proud and pleased with myself and what I did to help myself which took real determination on my part at 66years of age to start it. My comments to anyone reading is don't ever give up when you are determined to do something better for yourself and those around you.

Written Monday 10/10/ 2016

Something Does Not Seem Right

This was indeed a very difficult paper for me to write because all five of the examples were close to my heart. Indeed they are so close I spent a lot of time just trying to decide. I started the paper with two but when getting to the real need for saying what made it difficult for me, I just shredded them and tried again.

I hope by saying the things I write in this paper the persons who will be reading it and hearing it presented will realize as I finally did after trying for more than ten years to help a person and had very little success, I said, "No! I have gone as far as I can go in helping you as I can see no apparent success. You are on your own now May God bless and help in all you need in life. I do understand your reasons for why you did everything the way it always came out to be best for you.

I am sure in the back of your mind you must have realized it had to end as you didn't see nor understand at all how it was affecting me. I suppose it was partly, because of the way I was raised. The help I had gotten when I was having problems in school learning as a small child. Adjusting to being in school with the other children was very hard for me and my grades were not very good. The instructors having to spend a lot of time helping me in the early years with my classes.

But as the years progressed and my parents got the real help I needed I was the Valedictorian of my High School Class. With a little further help from many persons at the school and community I was able to come to Charleston to a School of Nursing that no longer exists. Finishing school there after three years I had earned a Certificate to be a registered Nurse.

This was not gained until I took a state test to become a Registered Nurse. After passing the test and working for a couple of years in a couple of areas in West Virginia I moved on to Indianapolis, Indiana and took classes at the Extension Center part of the Indiana University, Bloomington, Indiana. After six years I earned my degree in nursing from the university and then continued working there for several years as a Registered Nurse with a degree before returning to West Virginia.

Slant the picture of the story forward to the beginning of the story and you will find a person, namely me, after several years of working, meeting many different persons with problems in life. But the one particular one I worked with, I for some reason, felt she had been very severely mistreated for many reasons.

Like a blind person, I offered some assistance for the many problems. I didn't realize it would turn into more than ten years with many different types of episodes requiring more than I should have done. I realize now it was a big mistake to even start but I have learned a lot from my mistakes. I think in a sense it has helped me to become a better person for myself and for assisting others but not in the same way I was beginning to feel abused.

The things I want to tell my classmates is, as you grow and mature in life, try to always be a good and kind person with others but learn the technique of, "when to say no" and mean it. Especially if the situation appears to be never going to change and will always be a problem for you. Just walk away in any way you can to make it safe for you as well as others involved.

For goodness sake don't feel guilty nor let the harsh remarks that may be given to you for several years hurt you because you were trying to be kind to one in need and let the situation get out of control. I was educated in my church to always try to help those in need. But that concept of knowing when to say, NO! I cannot help you any further. You are now on your own completely.

Now! I would like to try to say the only stereotypes I could find in this writing were those persons who were somewhat abrupt speaking to me as I tried to help the individual. I suppose that is just life and some of the tough problems we all must face as we grow and learn ourselves.

Written Tuesday 8/23/2016

Send a Card

Remembering important days in the life of people can be a very important part of their life as well as yours.

Recently, I realized I had forgotten to send a birthday card to a friend. She and I often exchanged cards for important days of the year such as birthdays, Christmas, Easter, Thanksgiving and many others as well as those just at random. This had become a big part of our lives for several years.

When I realized I had forgotten, I thought, "Well it's been already two and half months so just forget it for this year and either telephone her or send a card of friendship." In my thoughts of this person and the length of time we had known each other and the simple practice of sending a card, I decided she would like it better if I sent a late birthday card and explained to her what happened and why I forgot.

I did as my thoughts guided me to do and learned in a card she sent me recently she had been having a lot of health issues. She was such a private person she kept a lot of such matters to herself. As she explained it to me, she just didn't want to bother other people with her problems and health, so she managed them as well as she could alone.

I also learned one of her daughters living in another state came and got her mother. Her daughter took her to her home after having her checked by many different doctors in this area first. This took about two months or more to be sure they were doing all they felt she needed to have done and properly diagnosed her symptoms and give orders and proper treatment before she left this area.

Yesterday, I received a thank you card from her in the area where she is now with her daughter and son in law. She explained how much she appreciated the remembrance of the card and the receipt of it. She said, "The card brightened her day and lifted her spirit to have someone from her home town to remember her with such gracious memories." She explained that her health is definitely much improved and she hopes to be coming back to West Virginia soon, but that will depend on the doctors there and their decisions of the health issues of whether she can come back to living alone as she is a senior citizen.

I was very pleased to learn that she liked where she was and that her daughter and son in law had been so kind to her and helped to make her feel comfortable and happy. This is so important for the public to recognize and realize the importance of how growing older into the senior life, people quite often can become depressed and life just simply leave them. Many times, these seniors will just sit at home and quietly do just the least they have to do, occasionally watch television or talk to someone on the telephone, or nap. They may take a short walk and maybe go to church if someone will come by their home for them.

They usually will just vegetate into the loss of the normal life they once had due to the lack of proper activity and socialization with other people. Their food and fluid intake will become very minimal which causes many problems such as too much weight loss, bowel and urinary tract loss which eventually can cause very serious problems. I thought of all these things plus much more regarding senior citizens and what happens to them as they grow older. I thought she is lucky that she has a daughter and son in law that cares about what is happening to her and what they must do to help her through this part of her life.

In the card she sent me she wants to come back to her home in West Virginia and be independent again. Common sense tells all of us we do what we have to do at times when we can no longer do what is socially the proper thing to do. It is a matter all persons realize as they begin to grow older and must face matters like, "what would I do if I fell and could not get to the telephone and call for help."

I know how I have planned my life to try to avoid some of the problems seniors face, but what about those who have no one to rely on? My point is try to be a good neighbor and subtly be aware of the senior citizens where you work, go to church, live, and any other parts of life that may affect them in some way.

Be aware if a problem similar to what I have discussed and of course many others occur may be present in their life. Try to make them feel you will not hurt them but will try to get the right kind of help for them, if a problem occurs.

By all means send a card occasionally, make a phone call and check on them. Take their dog for a walk if they cannot due to health reasons. Go grocery shopping for them. Empty the trash for them. Do some special cooking for them of what they like and follow their special diet if they are on one. Offer to help clean their house or parts of the living space if permitted by them.

All of these special amenities that we can offer to the senior will make the final days of their life much easier, decrease the episodes of depression seniors seem to get very easily due to their inability to function in later years. They are still persons. They are still human and deserve whatever we can do to help them make their final years, hours, or whatever time is granted them to make it easier to live.

It's always very important to make them feel comfortable, feel safe, and happy. I have thought so many times of the senior citizen that does not get the support and help they need as they finalize their years from local friends and family and even those who live distances away, how this must effect the individual emotionally, mentally, and socially. In all the ways of life as they have lived it before, when a final determination is made by those in authority and they are placed in a nursing home, they should be at ease. I personally can tell you as a registered nurse it gives me the shivers and cold chills. I wonder if there isn't some way better for all senior citizens that must go through this.

I suppose this brings me right back to the point of what I said briefly in this essay earlier. I suppose it is just an issue we all face and hope we are doing the right things for ourselves as the years proceed. And we can cross over to the great beyond with a feeling we did the best we could with what we had to do with as we lived our lives. We created very little problems for others who are younger and are also trying to help us and prepare for the time they will be facing these same problems.

That is just the way life is and we just must play cards with the greatest of masters of the Card Game and hope we are occasionally the winner of a few games to make it easier for us and those responsible for our own final affairs. Good luck to us all. When writing about the senior citizens and their problems I could not help but think about the persons who have serious problems which leave them with disabilities such as heart disease and stroke which are just two of many disabilities we must work with as nurses.

Since I worked for twenty years at the former West Virginia Rehabilitation Center before it closed, I have seen many different types of disabilities that need very detailed care 24/7 and 365 days of the year. I have thought many times of many of these persons and their disabilities and where are they now? Who cares for them and manages all the aspects of their life trying to make it better and bearable as they face every day?

I know this must sound like I am a griever of all such problems but if that is others perception of me then. GOOD. My points are coming through somewhere but I wonder if the right people are READING, LISTENING, or IF THEY EVEN CARE. If you are then PROVE it. I would like to see some articles or whatever means you choose through technology to let it be known to me and the general public what you are doing for these type persons who need to be shown more respect and understanding for their FINAL DAYS.

I believe as the famous Judge Judy, when she has her court room discussions with people she is trying for whatever the accusations. Don't hand me any famous or mouthy situations. I want proof and if you have no written research to prove your case get off of my report. Don't waste my time. I've more people to shake up a little and make them see the problems they create and the lack of good common sense you use in helping people I have seen written about in this report.

Yes. That is the way life is for all of us and that includes you, me, and everyone. We are responsible for these people and must see they are shown more respect and receive better care wherever they are located. If we don't care enough then we are wrong and we should be the one that has to suffer a little to maybe understand what they suffer. Well, now that I have Rang the Bells of Mercy for the senior citizens and those who have disability's maybe I should say Thanks one and all for what you have done to help these persons who need you so much.

I understand that life is rough for all of us at times and we don't have time to even do all we should do for ourselves and our own families. Sometimes it is necessary for us to find just a little time and do some research on some problems and do something about them. Form some special committees and have special meetings to try to get groups organized to see what the real problems are with certain groups with lots of complaints and do what is really necessary to get rid of the problems. These health issues are indeed very important to all who must be a part of them.

And so in closing this essay, I will say to one and all as the Great Bob Hope used to say to the military forces in war times, "Thanks for the Memory, and may God bless and help us all."

Written Tuesday 10/4/2016

Pearl Buck's Visit to Charleston, WV

Sometime during the first week of April, 1969, Pearl Buck visited the Diamond Department Store of Charleston, West Virginia. I heard the time she would be visiting on the evening television news several days before she came.

I decided I wanted to be there for the autographing of her books because she had always been a favorite author of mine. I knew she was a native of West Virginia and that was important to me. I also knew that she was a very important writer and was the first woman to win the Noble Peace Prize for Literature in 1938.

The night before I went to meet her and the autographing of her books, I was beginning to get very nervous. I realized what an important person she was from reading of several of her books, as well as many articles written about her in newspapers, magazines, and other places such as the television and radio media.

I did the usual routine of taking a shower, washing my hair and fixing it as I usually do at night. I got my clothes arranged for the next day and brushed my teeth. I still was somewhat nervous and couldn't seem to get my thoughts together of how I should respond to a person like her. I finally decided to get dressed and walk over to Kroger's grocery store, which was very close to where I live. I met several church friends and a nurse friend doing late grocery shopping the same as me. I returned to home and the walk as well as the meeting of friends and talking at the store had really helped me to be more relaxed and calm.

I went to bed and almost immediately went to sleep. I awoke after seven good hours of sleep feeling very rested and ready to meet the day and Pearl Buck. After having my breakfast, I got ready with all the morning routines of the process and left where I live walking to get to the bus stop on the corner. I was there about ten minutes ahead of the usual schedule. The bus did not arrive at the usual time and I was beginning to get very nervous, thinking it had come early that day and I missed it.

In about five minutes, I could see it coming and when it arrived, the driver said the bus he was driving broke down and he had to wait for another bus to be brought to get us to Charleston. We got to Charleston all right, but the Virginia Street bus that would take us near the Diamond Department store had already left. I started walking just as fast as my feet would go for a person my age of thirty-six years.

I remember thinking as I walked that distance of about one-half mile, what a story I would tell my friends when I would have to tell them I didn't get there in time to meet Pearl Buck. I could feel the frustration rising in my brain and all through my body. I began to get very nervous and began to ask God why this had to happen to me. I really wanted to meet her and get my two books she had written autographed.

I had gotten to my destination by that time, frustration, disappointment, nerves, tears and all. I entered the store glancing at the ladies, gloves, panties, hose, bras and God only knows what else. I then passed through the men's department and it was just the same old thing. I turned around and looked at the men's underwear saying, "ye gad's I want to know where the closest elevator is located. I didn't come to see a burlesque show by men and women's undergarments! Will someone show me the closest elevator to the fifth floor where Pearl Buck is supposed to be autographing her books for those interested?"

A young boy standing on the other side of the underwear where the men's shirts were heard me and directed me to the elevator. I pushed the button and the elevator was there so fast, I couldn't believe what I was seeing. It went up to the fifth floor just as quickly and the door very gently opened.

I stepped out and walked down the hall then entered the multipurpose room where Pearl Buck was seated doing the book signing. I noticed there were seven persons ahead of me in line. Pearl Buck did not rush anyone as they came to her desk. She spent time gently talking to each person. And, I noticed she took the hands of each person at her desk before they left, both male and female with special comments to them.

As, I got closer to her desk, I was beginning to get rather warm and started to take the coat off I was wearing and she looked over at me and said, "Don't take the coat off. It looks very nice on you."

I abided by her request and left it on. The coat was black with white sections at the collar and the lapels. It was a long coat down to below my knees. I remember her eyes were blue and she had snow white hair. As she sat in the chair doing the autographing the closer I got to the desk, I could see better. It appeared she was wearing a dark color like black, navy blue or something like that and her blouse or whatever she was wearing as an upper body garment with a skirt or possibly slacks was very snug to her neck such as a priest or pastor would wear.

Then it was my turn to meet her and get my books autographed. I first stood as she introduced herself to me and I likewise to her. She invited me to sit down in the chair across from her with us facing each other. She autographed my two books, "The Good Earth" and "My Several Worlds." Then she took my hands in hers and spoke quietly and softly to me saying, "Tomorrow is Forever."

She pressed her hands into mine, then gently let go and turned around to another person waiting to see her, speaking softly and very kind to the person. I got up from the seated position and left.

I remember when I got home after relaxing a while, I began to think how did she know as much as she appeared to know about me when she spoke to me as I sat there with my hands in hers. And, what did she mean by, "Tomorrow is Forever. You will understand when the time is right."

Written Tuesday 11/29/2016

Only the Owl Knows the Truth

I ask for answers, you gave me truth and mystery of life

Then it all became a feeling of oblivion

I listened carefully and tried to understand, but the learning block

Always seemed there forever and ever.

It took a great while for me to understand your way

Slowly each day 1 began to see how you were teaching.

The oblivion finally faded away, but not without tears and

A lot of reinforcement.

This is my story to each of you this day

Listen to the Owl and he will bring you the answer.

It may come as a prayer, song, or discussion

Or even a flower you like and attend.

Inside of God's way there are many perceptions of life

As we live it.

We must just listen and see with the third ear and eye.

Then the real mysteries of life will become very simple

To all who listen and see as they learn his great teachings.

So listen my friends one and all, only the Owl knows the real truth.

What our great creator wants us to learn.

Let each realize to respect one another in his beliefs

And strive for the best for each other

Then you will see all the oblivion will soon pass away

Written Sunday 9/13/2015

Honesty: What Does It Mean in Our Daily Living?

Two years ago, on a Sunday morning I was rushing from where I had parked my car outside the Dunbar Intermediate School to get to the First Presbyterian Church for choir practice and morning service.

It was a beautiful sun shiny day on April 22, 2013 and on the calendar at home later I noticed it was officially Earth. Day. This was enough knowledge to allow me a good feeling of life and its daily incidents we face each day. This being recognized I was not surprised of how I felt in regard to the following activities and comments between a lady going toward the Dunbar United Methodist Church and myself going toward the First Presbyterian Church of Dunbar.

I did not notice as I got out of the car and reached for my purse and music container that my morning pledge check to the church had fallen out of the side pocket of the purse which was one half zipped together.

As the other lady was getting ready to drive into the same area where I was parked she slowed her car for a few minutes to let me get out of my car close the door, check to be sure it was locked and move on out of the drive in area to park next to my car. She told me after she was able to catch me that she saw the check fall to the ground from my purse, but since she was not sure she waited until she got out of her car and inspected the area finding it was a First Presbyterian Church envelope with my name and church identification number on it.

I was moving along so fast by that time I had gotten past the house of Carolyn Paschal, the choir Director of the Dunbar United Methodist Church. The lady would not call out my name, but just said, "Lady wait! I think I found something that belongs to you." When she did get to where I was standing she asked for my name and I said "Gracie Lester." She then handed me the First Presbyterian Church envelope which she had been waving in the air at me as she tried to catch me and said, "this belongs to you."

She gave me her name in our hurried conversation and looked both directions for oncoming vehicles then hurriedly crossed the street smiling as she waved and went in the door at the Dunbar United Methodist Church.

Unfortunately, the exchange was so rapid, I cannot remember her name to send her a thank you card for her kindness and human way of managing the loss of mine. And also the pledge loss to the First Presbyterian Church of Dunbar.

The day was certainly very rewarding to me in many ways to meet a person like that and the activity it involved. It pleased me so much I wanted to write about the experience and let others perhaps feel some of the happiness and peacefulness I felt in her comments and activities of concern for me and my property.

I still was not satisfied therefore I wanted to do a little research and share it with you the readers. The references I have chosen to explain this further are:

1. Merriam Webster's Concise Dictionary:

A. Honest means feeling free from deception in life dealings with others.

B. Learning how to trust another in life's activities.

C. Being frank and making the person you are dealing with feel you are honest.

D. Honestly Used as an adverb in explaining something to another to indicate honesty.

E. Honesty used as a noun in sentence writing for understanding honesty.

2. The Living Bible:

A. Romans 12:17

The message is never pay back evil for evil. Do in such a way that everyone can see it.

B. Romans 13:13

The night is far gone, the day of his return will soon be here. Stop the evil deeds of darkness.

C. 2 Corinthians 8: 21

God knows we are honest, but I want everyone to know it. That is our arrangement.

D. 2 Corinthians 13: 7

I pray that we will all live good lives, not because that will put a feather in our caps, proving we teach what is right even if we ourselves are despised.

E. 1 Timothy 2:2

Pray in this way for kings and all others in high places of responsibility so we can live in peace and quiet, spending our time thinking about our lord.

Thank you again my mystery Dunbar United Methodist Church friend, for with your kindness and perceptive understanding of what you did that day, you got me interested in doing some research on what honesty means and how we should use it in our daily living practices. I hope we meet again sometime so that I can give you a proper thank you with a smile as you gave me when you walked into the church door that day April 22, 2013.

Yesterday's Dreams Mirrored Tomorrow

When returning from Indianapolis. Indiana on May 25th. 1965, I lived in a lifelong friend's home for twenty-two months in Dunbar WV until I could find employment and housing. Moving into an area where I had not lived for several years since I moved to Indianapolis, Indiana to begin my BS Degree in Nursing at the Indiana University Extension Center, I was having problems finding adequate housing and employment.

I am not sure why this was happening except all the business places I applied for employment, the Director of Nurses kept me waiting for a long period of time before finally saying the job I applied for was filled and they had nothing more to offer. Perhaps it would be better that I say one of the persons I did get an interview with was honest enough to say to me in a very kind way my evaluation from an employment in Indianapolis. Indiana stated that I had some personal problems at their place of business and they had to release me from their employment.

The evaluation, according to her stated I should get some special help for these problems. The lady is dead now, God rest her soul. At least she was the only one of more than 23 businesses I placed an application for employment that was willing to say she could not hire me because I had predisposed mental health problems.

She did not offer to help me to get any Psychiatric nor Psychological help. That was not the case in Indianapolis, Indiana. The Director of Nurses helped me to get an appointment with the hospital Psychologist and the Psychiatrist. Most of the discussions with them were just question and answer sessions regarding my family in WV and about my future goals since the breakup with my man. He did not do nor order any specific Psychological tests as is done this day and time.

The Psychiatrist was part of the hospital staff also. He always talked to me at his office within the hospital. It was mainly question and answer sessions. He never ordered any specific nor detailed tests to be done. Most of his treatments with me were symptoms I discussed with him. He had me taking Nembutal to help me to sleep for a brief period of time. At intervals he would change the drugs to Carbitrol, Seconal, Fiorinal, Tofranil, Equanil and others as needed.

I never had the opportunity to attend any of the clinics they had to offer in Indianapolis. Indiana for mental health but I was aware there were a few in those days with specially educated Psychiatric Counselors to help persons with mental health problems.

I never had the services of Electric Shock Therapy, nor any of the other such therapies offered for mental health problems but I did see them performed many times on clients when I worked on a Psychiatric unit for three years at one of my employments. I never had the opportunity to see a surgical procedure titled Lobotomy but I have taken care of clients who have had the frontal lobe of the cerebrum cut into or across as a treatment for certain types of severe psychoses. This was a surgical procedure done for very severe and uncontrollable mental health problems which could not be controlled through the more common methods of treatment.

When I did get the interview with the lady who said she could not hire me because of my mental health problems, I explained to her I was very much in need of a paying job. Even if it was a lesser paying job than a Registered Nurse, such as a Nursing Assistant or anything else she might have to offer, or she could guide me to somewhere in the hospital, a job that I could use to prove myself to the hospital Administrator and others of importance. I told her I very much needed some type work for an income and to have hospitalization and medical insurance.

I explained to her everywhere else I had applied I was refused even interview. And in several cases the Director of Nurses secretary got the job of telling me I was not wanted at their place of business.

She said, "I am very sorry Miss Lester, I can't do what you are requesting. It is against hospital policy. It would create confusion and dissatisfaction among the other employees here where you were placed to work. And as a Registered Nurse with all the different types of work you have done, there would definitely be friction for you and the other hospital employees."

I went to my friend's home from the interview feeling like the whole world was falling in on me. She asked me how the interview went, and I said nothing except not very well. I did not get the job. I felt very cold and tired and I had a great deal of difficulty just trying to make small talk. When dinner time came, I felt like I was choking to death just trying to swallow any of the food. I finally just stopped trying to eat, helped to clean the kitchen, and went to bed earlier than usual.

Time seemed to be at a standstill for about three days when I did finally get a phone call from the Director of Nurses at Charleston General Hospital. It was 6/13/65 the time and she explained to me she needed my services to cover for vacation time on several units during the summer. I went in at the time she chose, to her office and did all the paperwork. She started me to work the next day.

I covered the day, evening, or night shift as she requested for approximately six months. I learned through hospital gossip and the Director of Nurses there was a need for an instructor in the former Charleston General Hospital School of Nursing as a Clinical Instructor in Fundamentals of Nursing. I asked and learned from the Director of Nurses how to apply for the job. After about three weeks, I learned I had the job. I started on this job 1/30/1966 and it lasted until Friday, 9/29/1969.

That was the horrible day when I reported on duty as usual, went to my office and got the necessary items I would need to work with the students in the hospital for their actual patient assignments. I was ready to start out the door toward the hospital when the Director of Education came out of her office and stopped me. We exchanged the usual morning greetings but immediately I recognized something was amiss. The odor in the air was of fear and worry.

The look on her face was the same as one that had been beaten down verbally to a pulp. She explained I would not be going to work that morning but to the hospital Administrators Office. When I asked her, all she could tell me was the administrator had some questions he wanted to discuss with me.

I remember I felt numb all over and I couldn't feel my feet touching the ground as I walked over to the hospital from the education building. My hands were cold and in fact I felt cold all over. I got to the hospital and when walking down the hall to his office, I remember there were people passing me and speaking to me, but I could not recognize any of them by name, so I just said hello and went on.

When I got to his office I gently knocked on the door and he said in what sounded like a normal tone to "come in." I opened the door and immediately I saw sitting in a chair opposite where I was requested to sit the assistant administrator. This made me feel very uncomfortable because I was not told he would be there.

The frowning hospital administrator began the discussion after a brief and what sounded like a very grumpy hello to my greeting. I said I was sent here by the Director of Education who said you have some questions you want to ask.

He said, "Yes, I want to know have you been treated for mental illness?" He then placed my application for a job on the desk and where I could not see it.

I said, "I had mental health therapy when I lived in Indianapolis and lost my man. I had a nervous breakdown."

He said, "Why the hell don't you have it written on your application for a job here?"

I said, "Sir, if you will look very closely I filled in every blank on the application. There was no place for me to write it unless I wrote on the top, bottom, or the sides of the application. Both administrators got their heads together and could find no space for me to fill it in.

Then he glared at me and said, "Get the hell out of here. You are fired and if you don't get out right now, I will call the police to put you out." He then threw the application form across the desk at me.

I left as he requested after returning to the education building turning in my keys, and some other items I was instructed to return. The next morning on the front page of the morning newspaper was a third of the page with the long-expected announcement of the closing of the Charleston General Hospital School of Nursing with the graduation of the present three classes. And the final three of those classes graduated in June 1972. Also, on the front page of the morning newspaper was the official retirement announcement of the Charleston General Hospital Administrator, for the end of the year 1969.

He stated he had been planning it for a long time and believed this was a good time since the School of Nursing was closing and a lot of other big changes were coming for Charleston General Hospital. About two weeks after I left, I received a check from the secretary of the school of nursing with an amount I don't remember which supposedly represented the time I had worked and vacation time accrued for that time I had not been paid.

I looked it over and felt it was too much and I was just being bribed for someone's idiotic folly, especially after reading the newspaper article. I returned the check refusing to cash it saying I want only the amount I worked and nothing more. I don't appreciate people's trashy ways of doing things and that goes for corporations just to make a point. About a month later I got a different check with a smaller amount than before but nothing more.

Later I talked with a friend about this and nothing was said by her except that was probably my accrued vacation time. They probably do owe me a little vacation time which over the years of September 29th, 1969 to December 15th, 2009 amounts to forty years plus two months. But I want a long overdue apology from the brass before I will even talk to them about it. I suffered very deeply going through the nervous breakdown and it was several years of emotional pain, grief, remorse, disappointment, sadness, depression episodes, anxiety, fear, crying episodes and many other symptoms. I am not totally healed and probably never will be but at least I am going in the right direction.

It has been for me a long time. I will eventually write a book about the beginning of the relationship which essentially caused the breakdown and what it meant to me as it progressed. But. I want to learn to be a good writer before I attempt anything that big. In my heart and soul, I shall never forget the day he returned to get a few things he still had at my home. He kept showing me his left hand and the wedding band. He did not let me meet her. She stayed in the car downstairs while he was getting his things.

As he left, going down the steps where I lived in an apartment, he turned at the bottom of 15 hallway steps and looked back with great sadness in his face. I looked at him the same way I am sure because of how I felt. It was like in one brief moment we were transfixed in time for eternity. I suddenly gained enough strength to say, "Go on. She is waiting in the car for you all to start life together. You have a long drive yet to get there."

Written Tuesday 12/15/2009

The Possum Tale

Life goes on for all of us no matter what happens. We all must learn how to get through the ups and downs. This I know is a strange way to start a paper of any type we wish to write.

Allow me to explain how this one incident affected my very well-planned day I had for Saturday, August 8, 2015. I had many things planned to get done that day which would all take about one or two hours at least to do. On a random thought I decided I would take the trash out which I had allowed to gather in the back storage room for at least three days.

As I was placing the bags of trash in my placement area I could hear a strange sound coming from one of the cans opposite to mine with no lid on it. I looked inside the can and saw an animal with a long nose and face which had apparent tears in its eye's. The animal also had a long tail.

I wanted to reach down into the can and reposition the animal in some way to make it more comfortable but I was afraid it would bite, scratch, or attack me in some other way. I spoke very softly to the animal and told it I would be right back. I was going to get it some help.

Maybe it was just my imagination of feeling sorry for the animal because the sun was very hot coming down that day. I wanted to place a lid over the can in my thoughts, but I thought that would frighten the animal and cause it to have more anxiety. I came into my home and called the local fire department to try for help.

The man who answered said that is a possum. He gave me the number for the local police department as he said the fire department does not manage those type life matters. Instead the police would get in touch with the local humane officer and get the animal back to its place of residence.

A lady answered and said she would pass the information on to the humane officer, but she did not know how long it would take for them to come to this area to get the animal. I went back out to the trash area and spoke to the animal explaining, "I am trying to get someone to come and help you. Please give me just a little more time and I will get someone who knows how and what to do to help you." I couldn't believe my eyes, but I thought the animal was smiling at me as it turned its head toward me.

I did return and spoke to the same lady on the phone at the police department as it was already more than an hour I had been waiting for help to come. And going back and forth to talk to the animal and pacify it as it laid with the hot sun coming down on it. This time the lady told me the local humane officer had retired and this area was using services occasionally from some of the local areas. She gave me their phone numbers and I tried one area where they said they no longer did those type services for the other nearby areas. They did tell me I could call the State Department of National Resources, but if they sent someone there would be a cost.

I told them I would call my land lord and let him help me resolve the problem. Someone of all the persons I was discussing this with told me to turn the can over and let the animal just wander away as it chose. I said "No, we have a lot of children who ride their bikes up and down this street and play games. We also have senior citizens and those with disabilities which could be hurt or injured in some way if the animal was sick or rabid."

I called my land lord and he told me to put the lid over the can to keep the sun off of the animal and he would be down to help it He was here in a short period of time and took the animal out of the can placing it into a crate then transported it to the area behind the Dunbar Kroger's Store that has a fence around the river. He placed the animal over the fence and it wandered back toward the river.

He told me he could have sworn the animal when it turned and looked back smiled at him. It then turned and went down the slope to the river wagging its tail as it went.

The blessing and lesson of this story is don't forget the animals no matter what they are.

They need food, care, understanding, and a home where they can get this type care as the winter approaches and any other time when they are in distress. And for all the other persons who tried to help me as I tried to help the animal THANK YOU. You were not wrong in anything you told me to do nor in what you tried to do. You were just following the policy of your work place.

Imagination of Sound Perception
Angel Song

I heard the sound of an angel sing on a Sunday morning recently at church after the morning service. I turned my head to hear the sound more clearly as the echoes came flashing into the Parlor hallway where I was standing. I was checking the routine information on the bulletin board to keep myself up to date on the duties and activities of the church.

The sound of music and singing appeared to be coming from the sanctuary where there were adult workers cleaning the seats and arranging the area for the next necessary activity. I stood there for a few minutes listening to the resonance of the beautiful childlike voice never missing a beat of the song she sang.

I then walked through the coat room into the entrance way of the church and looked down the aisle to the cross. I could see in the area where the Pastor speaks. I saw a beautiful little bare footed girl walking erect and in precision as if she had been assigned to do this very performance.

She walked gracefully and purposely with something in her hands, open as if she was reading it. I watched her for a few moments as the workers around her continued their work of preparing the sanctuary for the next scheduled activity. The song she was singing was, Jesus Loves Me this I know, for the Bible Tells Me So.

With proper walking posture and never missing a word, she sang the whole song through by the time she got to the front of the church. She then turned as if she was facing the Congregation and I could see it was apparently the morning bulletin of activities we had just done for the day.

She was holding it open as if she had been reading the music from all the other activities of the day. I lightly clapped my hands to let her know not just verbally, but also with the sound of my hands telling her also she sang a beautiful song and she performed as a real professional in music.

She then ran from where she was standing to her great aunt, Cindy and Uncle Rick who were cleaning the sanctuary for further activities. Beth and others were present. It has been at least a month since I noticed this experience with our future Opera Star. I wanted her to hear it directly from me that I like the sound of her voice and the good possibilities of what the future may hold for her in music. It was a very calming experience for me to hear little Mya Jolie, one of our very own, singing in such perfection.

May God bless and guide you little angel in all that you may become in the future. May parents and other family members guide you in the way you wish to go. May the school system recognize your talents and how it can affect others making them feel better when for some reason or for many reasons they are feeling very much in need of your voice to cheer them up. May your voice keep them moving along in their own journey of life.

Written Wednesday, May 6, 2015

About the Author

Gracie Lester was born joyous on Indian Creek, Wyoming County, West Virginia some 85 years ago. She was one of the privileged students of those days to attend her first two years going to school in the one room schools where the students were grades one through eight.

As a youngster, she lived way out in the country and usually the teacher (he or she) would have eight to ten students. The oldest male students were the "maintenance crew" who did all the cleaning and making sure the pot belly stoves were stoked with wood or coal to keep everyone warm and comfortable.

After a couple years, Gracie was transferred to the Wyoming, West Virginia grade school where the coal company was located. She then attended Pineville Intermediate School and then four years at Pineville High School.

As her sister Hazel wrote in a newspaper article: "Gracie Lester was chosen "Miss Nightingale" by the student government association at the Charleston General Hospital School of Nursing 40 years ago.

The "Miss Nightingale" contest was judged by the students who nominate and elect their choice based on personality, intelligence, ability to get along with co-workers of different phases, leadership, and good judgment in all problems and attitude in class work.

Miss Lester went on to Indiana University and earned her Bachelor of Science degree in General Nursing. Today she works for the State of West Virginia in the rehabilitation program.

Miss Lester graduated from Pineville High School in 1952 with a four-year straight-A average. She is the daughter of the late Frank Edgel Lester of Indian Creek. Her mother, Josephine Morgan Lester, resides in Gladys, VA.